# How to Rule the Kitchen

*Handy hints and tips for*

*culinary excellence*

by Annette Hoogeweegen
*illustrated by Barbara Hoogeweegen*

Published by Honeybee Books
Broadoak, Dorset
www.honeybeebooks.co.uk

Copyright © Annette Hoogeweegen 2015
Images © Barbara Hoogeweegen 2015

The right of Annette Hoogeweegen to be identified as the author of this work has been asserted by her in accordance with the Copyright, Designs and Patents Act 1988.

No part of this book may be reproduced in any form or by any electronic or mechanical means including information storage and retrieval systems without permission in writing from the author.

The information provided in this book is designed to provide helpful information on the subjects discussed. The publisher and author are not responsible for any specific health or allergy needs that may require medical supervision and are not liable for any damages or negative consequences from any treatment, application or preparation, to any person reading or following the information in this book. This book is not meant to be used, nor should it be used, to diagnose or treat any medical condition. For diagnosis or treatment of any medical problem, consult your own physician.

Printed in the UK using paper from sustainable sources

ISBN: 978-1-910616-43-7

Annette ran her own catering business in London for 20 years catering for banks, insurance companies, private dinners and cocktail parties. Annette then moved to Wiltshire and started a wedding company organising and catering for large country weddings. At the same time Annette also taught cooking to ladies and business men. She did this with a master chef.

All the hints and tips in this book have been tested and used by Annette throughout her career.

hoogeweegena@aol.com

# Vegetables

Adding a little sugar or lemon peel to any green vegetable while cooking it will help keep the vegetable green.

# Potatoes

Roast potatoes can be prepared and cooked the day before which saves time and works well. Peel, leave whole, boil slowly, when nearly cooked drain, cut to the size you would like and transfer them to an oven pan that has hot beef, goose fat or oil if you prefer. Cook until turning a golden colour, drain from the fat, return to pan leave in a cool place (not in the fridge).

When required place pan in oven and cook till golden brown, the fat left on the potato will make it crispy, serve.

$\mathcal{A}$dd a little horseradish cream to mashed potatoes gives them a great added dimension. Delicious served with fish.

$\mathcal{L}$eft over new potatoes, chop how you wish mix with mayonnaise sprinkled with chopped chives.

$\mathcal{N}$ever throw away mashed potato. Freeze in a suitable container, then defrost to thicken soups.

$\mathcal{P}$eeling potatoes for salads is tedious, make a light incision on the circumference of the potato put into cold water cook until very nearly cooked, soft, drain put into iced water when cool enough to handle gently pull the skin it will easily slide off.

# Sprouts

Sprouts can be cooked the day before use. Cook in boiling water, do not overcook as they still need to be firm and crunchy, drain, plunge into iced cold water till cold. This keeps the sprouts green. Drain, cover with cling film, leave in a cool place.

When ready for heating, melt butter in a saucepan, add the sprouts and heat slowly through. They will retain their colour and finish cooking.

Left over sprouts: put into an oven proof dish, toss in your oil of choice then add sundried tomatoes. Delicious with chicken and pork.

# Beetroot

$\mathcal{D}$o not cut the tops and root too short before cooking otherwise they will 'bleed' in the cooking and not retain that fabulous colour. Put the beets in cold water bring to boil then simmer until cooked.

$\mathcal{L}$eave them to cool in the cooking water, use gloves to skin the beets otherwise you will have red fingers. The remainder tops and tails will come off. Great hot or cold or in a white sauce.

# Carrots

$\mathcal{N}$ew carrots are simple delicious roasted in the oven, top the carrots leaving a little green (looks good) melt butter in a frying pan, caramelise lightly and then put in a hot oven, when cooked sprinkle with grated parmesan.

# Asparagus

Do not cut asparagus ends, as there is a natural break between the hard and edible.

Trim the sides of the asparagus of their 'spiky' pieces with a sharp knife, plunge the asparagus spears into iced water for about 10 minutes, this will bring the chlorophyll to the surface and the spears will be a great green.

Put the spears in either a pan of hot water and simmer till tender, steam or put into a frying pan with butter and cook until tender or lay the spears on tin foil, drizzle with oil and scatter with grated parmesan roast until tender.

# Green beans

*(french beans)*

Top and tail, put into pan of boiling water, cook until still crunchy, drain, plunge into iced cold water. When cold drain and cover with cling film. When ready to use melt butter in a saucepan, toss in the beans, heat and serve. They will still retain their lovely green colour.

# Onions

Small button onions and shallots are awful to peel, if the recipe states keep whole for casseroles, which looks good, put onions unpeeled into a saucepan, pour on boiling water, cook for a few minutes, drain, leave to cool. The skins will then peel off easily.

When frying sliced onions heat butter or oil in pan, put in the onions to cook. Do not add salt as this takes out the moisture from the sliced onions and they will stew rather than fry.

# Avocados

Cut lengthways, take out stone, cut into quarters peel off skin, it makes neat pieces. If not using all the avocado leave the stone in and cover put in fridge it keeps better, but use within a day

# Celery

Wrap celery in tin foil before putting it in the fridge. It will last much longer and will not curl.

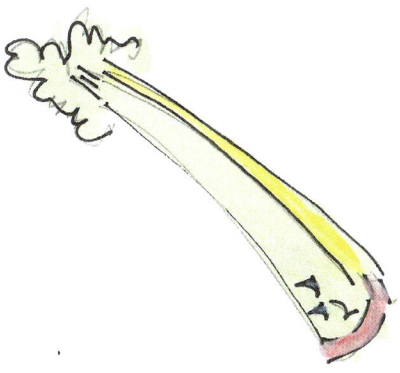

# Garlic

Roasted garlic is delicious, use large whole garlic, elephant garlic is great slice thinly the top off the garlic not the root end roast in the oven until soft  then squeeze the garlic and you will have a sweet garlic paste. If not using immediately put into the fridge

# Celeriac

A wonderful vegetable people are apprehensive about. Peel the celeriac and grate it. Put single or double cream into a large frying pan. Heat the cream, add the grated celeriac and heat through. Don't overcook.

Wonderful served with duck breast or fillet steak. This is just one of the ways to cook celeriac - it takes minutes.

# Tomatoes

Two methods of peeling tomatoes:

Freeze, defrost ; the skin will come off easily and will be good for sauces for pasta or stews.

*Or*

Plunge into hot water for a few minutes drain and cool. The skins will come off easily, and using this method the tomato will not be so soft.

# Bits of raw veggies

Bits and pieces of vegetables: Put in a bag in the freezer when you have collected enough. Cook in a small amount of water till tender, liquidise to use as a soup base, or strain to make veggie stock. Freeze in ice cube containers.

# Herbs

*A*ny leftover herbs: Chop finely, put into a jar with a little olive oil, shake, keep in a cool place. Great for stews, omelettes and sauces. You can also mix with melted butter in a ramekin then freeze. Chop the stalks finely to add to casseroles, as they have huge flavour. Herbs can also be frozen in ice trays with a little water can then be put straight from frozen into stews or soups.

# *Salad*

We all buy bags of salads, once opened they wilt and go off very quickly. By adding a piece of paper kitchen towel to the bag before returning to the fridge, you will enhance their lifetime! The paper absorbs the moisture which makes the leaves soggy.

# Lemons

*H*alf a lemon left over: slice into thin slices, put into a small freezer container, freeze, pop into your gin and tonic strait from the freezer!

*R*oll lemons on work surface with the palm of your hand this makes it easier for squeezing and produces more juice.Before squeezing take off some peel freeze good to use when cooking rice

*I*f the lemons have completely dried do not throw out, put the lemons into hot water. They will swell and be usable.

# Bananas

The bugbear of every kitchen: over ripe bananas. Peel, slice, put into freezer container, freeze. When you have a moment defrost and make ice cream!

Banana bread is also easy to make and freezes well.

# Soft fruit

When freezing raspberries, strawberries, gooseberries, put them on a tray in a single layer and freeze. When completely frozen put them in freezer bags.

To defrost spread out on a tray. They will defrost very quickly and not be squishy.

# Bread

If not sliced roughly do so. Put into hot oven that is no longer required but still hot, brown, leave to cool, put into magimix or same. When the crumbs are fine enough for coating your fish or chicken put into a container and store in cool dry place.

Sliced stale bread:

To make croutons cut into squares, fry in oil tossing continuously, drain on paper towel, freeze, delicious for soups or salads.

# Cheese

Any bits and pieces of cheese: grate, put in freezer bag, freeze. Use the cheese in omelettes, sauces etc. from frozen.

# Meat

All meat joints should be sealed before roasting, as this keeps in the juices.

If you are putting garlic or rosemary into the joints, do this before sealing. Make a small slit in the meat and insert the garlic or rosemary, then seal as follows. In a large frying pan or oven tin, put in some fat, (dripping or oil whatever you wish). Heat, then add the meat joint and seal the sides, turning all the time. Do not forget the ends of the joint. When sealed, season, put into oven to roast. The sealing can be done the day before, in order to save time on the day itself.

When sealing meat for casseroles or curries using beef, lamb or chicken, dice the meat and put it into a plastic bag with flour, pepper and salt and toss. Make sure that all the diced meat is coated. This saves a mess on your work surface. Take the meat out and dispose of the bag. Then seal the meat as recipe states.

Tossing in flour will also help thicken the jus in the casseroles.

# Chicken

$\mathscr{I}$f you have bought a chicken and you are short of time to cook the whole chicken, cut off the legs and wings and freeze, or cook with the breast for cold the next day. Mix herbs of your choice into softened butter, lift the skin on the breast and push in the softened butter. Then massage to spread under the skin and cook in a medium oven. This takes half the time to cook.

# Fish

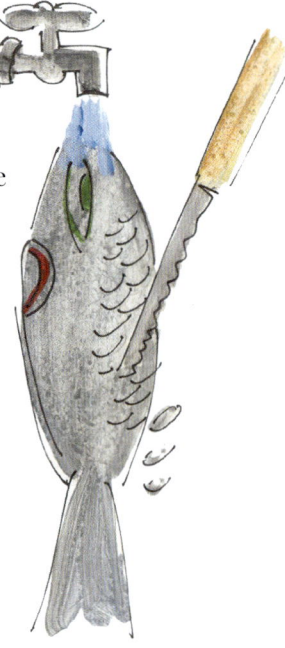

When preparing small fish for grilling or barbecues, skewer three or four together through the heads. They then do not disappear into the charcoal.

If the fish is very scaly hold the fish under the tap by the tail and scrape downwards towards the head with a blunt knife. Rinse well and pat dry with a kitchen towel.

# Baking whole fish

There are several methods of baking fish.

Wet three to four sheets of greaseproof paper and wrap the fish in it one sheet at a time, then finish by wrapping in wet newspaper. It takes about five mins for the heat to penetrate the paper then cook the fish as the recipe dictates. Round fish takes longer than flat fish, the skin usually comes off when unwrapping the fish.

*Or*

Put whole fish on a large sheet of foil that has been brushed with lots of melted butter and scrunch up the foil at the sides to make a canoe shape. Prepare a mix of melted butter with tarragon or a herb of your choice, pour this into the fish cavity, seal the foil and bake in a hot oven for approximately 30 mins.

*Or*

Whisk an egg white until stiff. Fold in course salt and coat the fish with the mixture, then bake. The salt crust will go hard and break away from the fish when cooked.

# Fish steaks

Put the fish skin side down in hot oil or butter or a mix of both, cook till skin is crispy then turn over to cook for the last few minutes, serve skin side up. I love the crispy skin.

## Grilling

Cover the grill pan with foil help cook the fish more evenly and you do not have a messy grill pan to clean!

# Mussels

Wash the mussels thoroughly under a running tap, pull off any rope pieces stuck in the shells. If any of the shells are even a bit open tap them firmly. If they do not close, throw them away and then proceed as the recipe states.

# Eggs

If you hate touching raw eggs when separating, crack the egg into a bowl, take a small empty plastic water bottle, put the top over the yolk, and squeeze the bottle to suck up the yolk. Then squeeze the yolk out into another bowl! Use as the recipe states.

Egg whites:

Put them in ice trays, freeze. Defrost, use at room temperature, never refreeze. Uses: meringues and mousses.

Left over yolks store in the fridge for only 2 days, covered with cling film. Great for making homemade mayo.

When boiling eggs add salt to the water this stops the shells from cracking.

# The perfect poached egg

Line a small ramekin with cling film, oil the cling film lightly. A small freezer bag can be used instead. Put a little butter in, break in the egg, tie the cling film or freezer bag, leave air in the cling film or bag so it will float. Lift it out of the ramekin and put into boiling water that is moving gently for about 3 minutes (or however runny you wish your egg). Take the package out and just push the egg with your finger to test if it is cooked enough for you. .

If you wish to cook several eggs take the eggs out of the hot water slightly earlier, plunge into cold water in the bag or cling film, (which ever method you are using). When required put into slowly boiling water for one minute to heat through.

When cooked to your liking take the package out of the water, cut the cling film or freezer bag just under where you have tied it and turn out the perfect egg. Delicious with fresh asparagus or on toast with poached haddock.

# Souffle dishes

Make sure you grease well, the top of the dish as well as the inside. This will help the soufflé to rise and not get caught on the rim.

# *Cream*

When using cream to fill a meringue roulade or a pastry requiring to be filled with cream, whisk the cream lightly and add some lemon curd (to your taste). Whisk in. This gives the cream an extra dimension, delicious.

# Rice

When cooking rice add a few drops of lemon juice to the water this 'bleaches' the rice and helps the grains not to stick together. When the rice is cooked place a damp cloth over the pan leave for a few minutes. The rice will not be soggy. This tip came from a Philippino friend.

# The Benefits of Flour

Some time ago, I was cooking some sweetcorn and stuck my fork in the boiling water to see if it was ready. I missed and my hand went into the boiling water! A friend of mine, who was a Vietnam veteran, came into the house as I was screaming, and asked me if I had some plain old flour...

I pulled out a bag and he stuck my hand in it. He told me to keep my hand in the flour for 10 minutes. He told me that in Vietnam he had seen a guy who had caught fire and in their panic people had thrown a bag of flour all over him to put the fire out...Well, it not only put the fire out, but apparently he never even had a blister!

... Long story short, I put my hand in the bag of flour for 10 mins, pulled it out and did not even have a red mark or a blister & absolutely NO PAIN.

Now, I keep a bag of flour in the fridge* for when I burn myself.

Try it . . . Experience a miracle!

Why not keep a bag of flour in your fridge, you will be happy you did! Flour has heat absorbent property and also has a strong antioxidant property, thus it helps in burn patients if applied within 15 minutes.

*Cold flour feels even better than room temperature flour.

# Household Tips

## Duvets

When struggling to put on the duvet cover, turn the cover inside out, put your hands in the cover, hold the two top corners, take the two corners of the duvet and shake the cover down, quick and efficient.

## Cashmere and wool

Always turn inside out when machine washing, this helps to stop the 'balling'.

## Washing machine

When the washing powder drawer gets clogged up, take it out and put it in the dishwasher. Wash normally with your dishes - all the old powder gone! Brilliantly clean.

Once a year or twice a year, depending on use, clean the washing machine by adding a bottle of white vinegar and putting the machine on a hot wash. This will help clean the machine and your washing will then be cleaner and fresher.

## Kettles

Do not buy expensive de-furrers, instead fill the kettle with a mix of ½ water and ½ vinegar, bring the mixture to the boil, empty the kettle and rinse it. You will have a lovely clean kettle!

## Microwave

If your microwave is looking grimy, put a little water in a microwavable container. Squeeze a lemon , add water to the lemon skins, microwave for a few minutes on full power , this will loosen any food stuck . The microwave can then be more easily cleaned.

## Homemade Mosquito spray

16 oz bottle
4 tsp vanilla extract
15 drops lavender oil
1/4 cup lemon juice

Put the mix in a bottle, give it a good shake then fill bottle with tap water, shake again, this works for most of the time.

## Soup

If you over salt soup drop in a peeled potato it will absorb the salt.

## Chilli peppers

When preparing chilli peppers rub your hands in vegetable oil this stops the chilli oil getting into your skin.

## Small cuts

If you nick yourself wait for the bleeding to stop cover the dry wound with clear nail polish it will not come off and fall into other dishes you are preparing

## Wooden Spoons.

Wooden spoons have many uses but this is the best tip and it works. Boiling any liquid in a pan, with pasta, rice etc lay a wooden spoon across the unlidded pan and it will not boil over.

## Knives

Never put your beautiful and sharp knives in your dishwasher as this will blunt them.

# Wasps

When having a barbecue in the summer wasps can be a nightmare and very unpleasant. Throw some pure coffee (not instant) grounds onto the charcoals. Wasps hate the smell and vanish.

No barbecue but lunch in the garden? Mix ground coffee with sawdust, put on a metal or heat proof plate and light. The wasps will vanish. Wasps hate the aroma given off by burning coffee grounds.

# Barbara Hoogeweegen

*Biography*

MA in Fine Art
City and Guild School of Fine Art
Kennington London 2010

Heatherleys School of Art
Winner of Best Artist Award 1997

University of East Anglia

Marchutz School of Art
Aix en Provence

Worked as a portrait painter 1997 – 2008

http://www.bhoogeweegen.com/
b.hoogeweegen@btinternet.com